The Easter Feast

Celebrate the Resurrection with Some New
Recipes That Will Revive the Whole Family

BY

MOLLY MILLS

License Notes

An Amazing Offer for Buying My Book!

Thank you very much for purchasing my books! As a token of my appreciation, I would like to extend an amazing offer to you! When you have subscribed with your e-mail address, you will have the opportunity to get free and discounted e-books that will show up in your inbox daily. You will also receive reminders before an offer expires so you never miss out. With just little effort on your part, you will have access to the newest and most informative books at your fingertips. This is all part of the VIP treatment when you subscribe below.

SIGN ME UP: *https://molly.gr8.com*

Table of Contents

Recipe 1: Smoked Salmon Flaky Bites

Smoked salmon could be served on Good Friday since it is fish of course! Combine with eggs and perhaps fresh green veggies and red onions and you are set with a wonderful lunch, breakfast or even an appetizer dish.

List of Ingredients:

- Phyllo dough
- ½ pound smoked salmon
- ¼ sliced red onion
- ½ package chives cream cheese
- 4 eggs
- 2 Tablespoons capers
- Pinch of salt and pepper
- Olive oil

Yield: 4-6

Cooking Time: 40 minutes

AAAAAAAAAAAAAAAAAAAAAAAAAAAAAAAAAAAAAAAAAAAAAAAAAAA

Instructions:

Preheat oven to 400 degrees F.

Get the phyllo dough out and lay it on a greased baking sheet.

In a skillet, heat the olive oil and cook for 5 minutes the red onion. Set aside.

Spread the chives cream cheese on the phyllo dough and then start assembling.

Place the smoked salmon, red onion, and capers.

Then crack 4 eggs at strategic spots on the phyllo dough, not too close to the edges.

Season everything with salt and pepper and bake in the oven for approximately 20 minutes.

Before removing the bites from the oven, try making sure that the eggs a fully cooked.

Serve with lemon wedges.

Recipe 2: Very Nutritious but Simple Pasta Salad

A pasta salad is always a life savior. No matter what time of the year, what occasion, Easter included, you will please the crowd without giving yourself a headache to find the most delicious but complicated recipe. This one is simple and easy to make, so if you have left over ham, turkey, chicken or even want to open a few cans of tuna, you can have a pasta salad ready to go in 20 minutes.

List of Ingredients:

- 1 package of shells pasta or other of your choice
- 1 cup cooked ham
- ¼ cup cooked crumbled bacon
- 2 cups broccoli florets
- 1 cup chopped yellow squash
- 2 minced green onions
- ¼ cup roasted sunflower seeds
- 2 cups mayonnaise
- 2 Tablespoons Sriracha sauce
- 1 cup crumbled blue cheese or Feta cheese (your preference)

Yield: 4-6

Cooking Time: 1 hour

AAAAAAAAAAAAAAAAAAAAAAAAAAAAAAAAAAAAAAAAAAAAAAAAAA

Instructions:

First of all, prepare the pasta by following the instructions you find on the package or box. Drain well and set aside.

Meanwhile, mix the Sriracha sauce, mayonnaise together and set aside also.

Cook your bacon and set aside to cool down and crumble as soon as it is perfectly cooked.

In a large mixing bowl, dump in the cooked pasta, chopped broccoli, green onions, yellow squash, bacon, ham and sunflower seeds.

Add the sauce and combine really well.

Finally add the crumbled cheese before serving.

Enjoy!

Recipe 3: Delightful Spring Salad

Easter lunches do not have to be super heavy and unhealthy. While you need to sometimes cook and feed many people, you can easily opt to prepare a healthy and nutritious salad. It's all about the ingredients, their freshness and the marriage of colors. Happy Easter!

List of Ingredients:

- 4 hardboiled eggs
- 4 -6 cups mixed greens
- 2 cups cubed watermelon
- 1 cup sweet kernel corn
- 4 small sliced radishes
- 2 medium sliced carrots
- ½ cup pearl onions

Vinaigrette:

- 1 tablespoon honey
- 2 Tablespoons balsamic vinegar
- ½ cup sesame oil
- 2 Teaspoons sesame seeds
- 2 Tablespoons chopped fresh cilantro

Yield: 4

Cooking Time: 1 hour

AAAAAAAAAAAAAAAAAAAAAAAAAAAAAAAAAAAAAAAAAAAAAAAAAA

Instructions:

First, proceed to cook the hardboiled eggs as you normally would in hot water and salt. Set aside when done and slice.

Then, prepare all the other ingredients, fruits and veggies.

In a bowl, mix the honey, vinegar, sesame oil, sesame seeds and fresh cilantro. You now have prepared your vinaigrette.

Time to assemble.

Lay a bed of fresh greens on 4 individual plates and add watermelon, kernel corn, radishes, carrots and pearl onions. Also, add a few pieces of hardboiled eggs.

Pour the vinaigrette reasonably on top of the salad and enjoy!

Recipe 4: Awesome Dinner Casserole

If you cooked chicken or turkey and you have some left over, then you have to be ready to make this dish. This recipe includes healthy ingredients, veggies, dairy products and grains.

List of Ingredients:

- 2 cups cooked turkey or chicken - your choice
- 2 cups tri-colored cooked quinoa
- 1 chopped large carrot
- 2 cups trimmed green beans
- ½ cup chopped red onion
- 3 minced cloves garlic
- 1 tablespoon olive oil
- 1 can cream of chicken
- 2 cups whole milk
- Salt, pepper
- Pinch of cumin

Yield: 4-6

Cooking Time: 2 hours

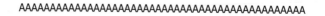

Instructions:

You can decide to use the slow cooker or oven for this recipe, I personally prefer the slow cooker, it's easy and it makes the house smell awesome!

In a skillet, cook the onion, garlic for about 5 minutes.

In a bowl, mix the milk, cream of chicken and salt, pepper and cumin.

Add the creamy mixture with garlic, onion and all the other ingredients into the slow cooker.

Mix to combine well and set on low temperature for about 2 hours. Serve when ready.

Recipe 5: Authentic Sweet Potatoes Casserole

There are many versions of a sweet potatoes casserole and sometimes in my family we will even have them blindfolded for the kids judge their favorite. You can use whipped cream, marshmallows or both. I actually prefer when it is not extremely sweet unless I plan to serve it as a dessert.

List of Ingredients:

- 5 or 6 large sweet potatoes
- 1 cup brown sugar
- ¼ cup coconut milk
- ½ cup unsalted butter (room temperature)
- 1 teaspoon almond extract
- 1 teaspoon cinnamon
- ¼ cup chopped walnuts
- 1 cup rolled oats
- 1 cup small marshmallows

Yield: 6-8

Cooking Time: 1 hour

AAAAAAAAAAAAAAAAAAAAAAAAAAAAAAAAAAAAAAAAAAAAAAAAAA

Instructions:

Preheat oven to 425 degree F.

Grease a large rectangle baking dish and set aside.

Cook the sweet potatoes in the oven for about an hour and peel after.

If you are in a hurry, you could also decide to cook the potatoes in the microwave for about 15 minutes and peel them after.

Either way, you will peel the potatoes and place them inside in a large mixing bowl.

Add to the potatoes: butter, coconut milk, almond extract, brown sugar and cinnamon. Use the electric mixer to make the mashed potatoes.

Pour all the mashed potatoes in the baking dish.

Sprinkle the rolled oats, the chopped walnuts and marshmallows.

Place the dish back and cook for another 30 minutes.

Serve warm.

Recipe 6: Cheesy Baked Casserole

I think everyone has to default to a cheesy casserole once in a while and why not use Easter as the perfect occasion to do so. You can start this recipe from scratch and bring to life this very yummy and cheesy casserole during your Easter break and enjoy it as a family.

List of Ingredients:

- 1 package penne pasta
- 2 cups sharp Cheddar cheese
- 1 large seasoned crushed tomato
- 2 cups shredded cooked turkey or chicken
- Pinch of salt and pepper
- 1 tsp dried oregano
- 3 minced cloves garlic
- 1 chopped green bell pepper
- 2 Tablespoons tomato paste
- 2 Tablespoons brown sugar

Yield:4-6

Cooking Time: 1 hour

AAAAAAAAAAAAAAAAAAAAAAAAAAAAAAAAAAAAAAAAAAAAAAAAAAA

Instructions:

Preheat oven to 375 degrees.

Cook the penne pasta as you normally would, according to the instructions on the package or box.

Grease a large rectangle dish and pour the pasta in it and also pour the crushed tomatoes.

In a skillet, heat some olive oil and cook for 10 minutes the garlic and green bell pepper.

You will add these cooked veggies next to the casserole and also the tomato pasta. Stir very well.

Finally add seasonings: salt, pepper, oregano and a little bit of brown sugar.

Stir in the cooked chicken or turkey and complete the casserole with a layer of Cheddar cheese.

Bake in the oven for about 25 minutes or until the cheese is melted and golden.

Serve warm with sour cream.

Recipe 7: Very Simple Breakfast Casserole

Let's make this simple but delicious casserole in the morning. Your guests, who spent the night at your house during the Easter break, will be pleased to wake up to the smell and goodness of this casserole. You can choose to cook it in the oven or you can also use the slow cooker to do so.

List of Ingredients:

- 5 large eggs
- 1 cup cornmeal
- 1 teaspoon garlic powder
- ½ tsp baking powder
- 2 minced green onion
- 1 cup diced cooked ham
- 2/3 cup whole milk
- 1/3 cup Greek yoghurt
- Pinch of salt pepper
- ½ cup shredded Cheddar cheese

Yield: 6

Cooking Time: 4 hours

AAAAAAAAAAAAAAAAAAAAAAAAAAAAAAAAAAAAAAAAAAAAAAAAAA

Instructions:

In a first bowl, mix the large eggs, whole milk, Greek yoghurt, salt, pepper, shredded Cheddar cheese and green onions.

In a different bowl, mix the cornmeal, garlic powder, baking powder.

Combine both mixtures and add cooked ham.

Pour the mixture into the slow cooker or crockpot.

Cook on low temperature for about 4 hours.

When cooked, serve with hot sauce of your choice.

Recipe 8: Warm Brie with Fruit Surprise

If you would like to fancy up your appetizer, try this warm brie with a fruit topping. I developed a taste for brie at a young age since my father was an absolute cheese lover and he would always come back from the market with 2 or 3 types of cheese to taste on the weekend, including Brie.

List of Ingredients:

- 1 large round Brie cheese piece
- 1 cup fresh raspberries
- 1 cup fresh cranberries
- ¼ cup orange juice
- 1 tablespoon orange zest
- 3 Tablespoons brown sugar
- Pinch of nutmeg
- Roasted pecans (optional topping)

Yield:6-8

Cooking Time: 1 hour

AAAAAAAAAAAAAAAAAAAAAAAAAAAAAAAAAAAAAAAAAAAAAAAAAA

Instructions:

Preheat oven to 375 degrees.

In a medium saucepan, mix the raspberries, cranberries with the orange juice, orange zest, brown sugar and nutmeg. Mix well and bring to a boil.

Once it is boiling, remove from the stovetop and get ready to pour on top of the brie.

First place the brie cheese on a greased dish and then pour the berries mixture generously on top.

Add the pecans on top and place the whole thing in the oven for about 10 minutes.

If you think it's taking too long, or you are in a hurry to serve to your guests, place it on broil but watch it closely because it will only take a few mines to get ready.

Serve with French baguette crackers and enjoy.

Recipe 9: Colored Mashed Potatoes

This side dish will definitely make a statement and will beautifully fill up any plate for Easter dinner. The focus will be on the colors of the potatoes and veggies but of course we will also pay attention to the taste provided.

List of Ingredients:

- 6 large white potatoes
- 2 cups broccoli florets
- 1 cup rutabaga
- 1 cup red cabbage
- 6 minced cloves garlic
- 3 Tablespoons butter
- 1 cup whole milk
- ¼ cup unsalted butter
- Pinch nutmeg
- Pics of salt pepper

Yield: 6

Cooking Time: 1 hour

AAAAAAAAAAAAAAAAAAAAAAAAAAAAAAAAAAAAAAAAAAAAAAAAAAAA

Instructions:

Boil the water and cook all the potatoes. I find it always much easier when they are cut into smaller pieces. You should prepare the rutabaga and also cook it in the same saucepan.

Meanwhile, cut the red cabbage and start steaming or boiling it.

In a third saucepan, you will also cook the broccoli and set aside when done.

When all the veggies are cooked, get ready for the next step.

In a skillet, heat some butter and cook the garlic.

Use 3 different mixing bowls. Divide the white potatoes equally and then add the red cabbage in one, the broccoli in the other, the rutabaga in the last one.

Divide also the cooked garlic in the 3 bowls.

Add some milk and butter to each bowl mixture, salt, pepper and nutmeg.

Proceed to mix with the electric mixer each one, until the mixture is smooth or when you are pleased with the consistency.

Serve a small portion of each colorful mixture in each guest's plate.

Enjoy!

Recipe 10: No Crust Mini Veggies Quiches

What a smart way to serve your guests a simple breakfast or brunch on Easter Sunday. If you are worried of having too much carbs then there is no need to worry since, this recipe does not call for a crust.

List of Ingredients:

- 5 large eggs
- ½ cup cottage cheese
- 1 cup shredded Mozzarella cheese
- 2 cups chopped spinach
- ½ cup chopped red onion
- 2/3 cup soy milk
- Pinch of salt and pepper

Yield: 12

Cooking Time: 1 hour

AAAAAAAAAAAAAAAAAAAAAAAAAAAAAAAAAAAAAAAAAAAAAAAAAA

Instructions:

Preheat oven to 400 degrees F.

Grease a 12 muffins pan, with some non-stick spray oil. Set aside.

In a skillet, heat a little olive oil and cook for 10 minutes the red onion with the spinach. Add salt and pepper, and set aside.

In a bowl, mix the eggs with cottage cheese and soy milk with a little of salt and pepper.

Next add the mozzarella cheese and the cooked veggies and mix all ingredients again together.

Pour into the 12 holes equally and make sure it does not overflow.

Bake in the oven for about 40 minutes and serve immediately.

I think my guests like when I put the hot sauce on the table to eat with the mini quiches or you can serve with a variety of condiments to choose from.

Recipe II: Traditional Easter Glazed Brioches

This is super traditional. These brioches are awesome to serve as a side with soup, ham or turkey. If you add some icing on top of the brioches, you will then have a delicious dessert or breakfast item.

List of Ingredients:

- 1 cup warm water
- 2 tablespoons quick rise yeast (your favorite brand)
- 2 tablespoons vanilla protein powder
- 2 cups all-purpose flour
- 1 egg
- 1 teaspoon baking powder
- ½ teaspoons baking soda
- 1 tablespoon olive oil
- ½ teaspoons nutmeg
- ½ teaspoons cinnamon
- 1 cup chopped dates
- Glaze for brioches
- 1/3 cup water
- 3 Tablespoons confectioner's sugar

Yield: 8-10

Cooking Time: 1.5 hour

AAAAAAAAAAAAAAAAAAAAAAAAAAAAAAAAAAAAAAAAAAAAAAAAAAAAA

Instructions:

Grease a large rectangle baking dish and set it aside.

In a mixing bowl, mix the water with the yeast and let it sit.

Add next, the protein powder and eggs and combine well.

Finally, add half of the all-purpose flour and combine until the batter is smooth.

Cover the bowl and let it rest for about 40 minutes.

Preheat the oven to 400 degrees F.

Add the olive oil and mix to the resting mixture and then add spice and raisins.

The dough should be ready to work with now.

Add a little flour on the working surface and start rolling.

Divide into 12 rolls or balls and then add the individual balls to the greased dish.

Bake for about 30 minutes or until golden.

Meanwhile, prepare the glaze by mixing together the water and confectioner's sugar and glaze once the brioches are slightly cooled down.

Recipe 12: Easter Turkey Meatloaf

Cooking meatloafs are so simple and easy to make, you can add the ingredients you prefer, the spices you prefer, the herbs you prefer so it is tailored to your liking.

List of Ingredients:

- 1-pound ground turkey
- 4 eggs
- ¾ cup Italian seasoned breadcrumbs
- 2 Tablespoons sweet relish
- 1 teaspoon yellow mustard
- ½ cup sour cream
- Pinch of salt and pepper
- Smoked paprika
- 1 chopped small yellow onion
- 3 minced cloves garlic

Yield: 4 -6

Cooking Time: 1.5 hour

AAAAAAAAAAAAAAAAAAAAAAAAAAAAAAAAAAAAAAAAAAAAAAAAAAA

Instructions:

Preheat oven to 375 degrees.

Grease the loaf pan and set aside.

In a very large mixing bowl, start mixing the following Ingredients: breadcrumbs, ground turkey, yellow mustard, sour cream, salt pepper, paprika and onion, garlic. Use your hands to really mix well if you don't mind getting your hands dirty since it does a great job mixing all of the ingredients together.

Next, add the sweet relish, mix again.

Place half of the meatloaf mixture in the pan and then crack the 4 eggs in the middle. Season with salt and pepper and cover with the rest of the meatloaf mixture.

Bake in the oven for at least 50 minutes.

Serve warm and with a sauce if you prefer. Enjoy!

Recipe 13: Cute Lemon Easter Cake

Not only will this lemon cake pleasantly surprise you, but it will also be enjoyed by your kids because of the candies you will use for this recipe. It is known that the kids love candies, colors and cake so this is a winning combination for sure!

List of Ingredients:

- 2 cups coconut flour
- ½ cup coconut palm sugar
- 1 teaspoon baking powder
- Pinch of salt
- 2 large eggs
- 1 cup sour cream
- 1/3 cup unsalted butter (room temperature)
- 1 cup coconut milk
- 1 teaspoon vanilla extract
- ¼ cup lemon juice
- 2 Tablespoons lemon zest
- ¼ cup Sprite (soda)
- 1 cup pastel color M&M candies

Yield: 8+

Cooking Time: 1 hour

AAAAAAAAAAAAAAAAAAAAAAAAAAAAAAAAAAAAAAAAAAAAAAAAAA

Instructions:

Preheat the oven to 375 degrees F.

Grease a square cake pan and set aside.

In a first large mixing bowl, combine the coconut sugar with the salt baking powder, coconut flour and coconut sugar.

In a second bowl, mix the eggs, sour cream, butter, coconut milk, and vanilla, lemon juice and lemon zest.

Combine both mixtures together. Add the Sprite and also candies.

Pour into the cake pan and bake for 40 minutes. Serve and enjoy!

Recipe 14: Yummy Baked Salmon

Baking salmon for Easter is a great idea. Serve the salmon filets with a fresh steamed green veggie and perhaps a quinoa based stuffing and you are in for one of the healthiest Easter ever.

List of Ingredients:

- 4 salmon filets with skin
- 2 cups trimmed asparagus
- ½ cup white dry white
- 3 tablespoons lime juice
- 4 minced cloves garlic
- Pinch of salt and pepper
- 2 Tablespoons Dijon mustard
- Fresh chopped parsley and chives or cilantro
- A drizzle of olive oil

Yield: 4

Cooking Time: 1 hour

AAAAAAAAAAAAAAAAAAAAAAAAAAAAAAAAAAAAAAAAAAAAAAAAAAAA

Instructions:

Preheat oven to 400 degrees

Clean each salmon filet individually and place them skin down in a greased baking dish.

In a skillet, heat the olive oil and cook the garlic. Add the lime juice and the wine. Also add the Dijon mustard and stir so it's well combined.

You will pour this sauce on top of your salmon filets.

Add the asparagus with the fish.

Add a pinch of salt and pepper on top of the asparagus and some fresh herbs.

Bake in the oven for about 25 minutes and serve warm with a side of brown rice or quinoa.

Recipe 15: The Perfect Herbs and Cream Scalloped Potatoes

This very yummy potatoes side dish will request make your friends and family ask for seconds. We are very confident, because this recipe has been tasted by our guests over the years and each time, we get showered with compliments and will eventually ask for more.

List of Ingredients:

- 2 large sweet potatoes
- 2 large white potatoes
- 2 Tablespoons unsalted butter
- Salt, pepper
- 2 minced cloves garlic
- 2 cups heavy cream
- ½ cup vegetables broth
- 2 cups ricotta cheese
- 2 cups shredded Swiss cheese
- ¼ cup mixed fresh chopped cilantro, chives, parsley, oregano, thyme,

Yield: 4-6

Cooking Time: 1.5 hour

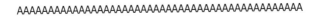

AAAAAAAAAAAAAAAAAAAAAAAAAAAAAAAAAAAAAAAAAAAAAAAAAA

Instructions:

Preheat oven to 380 degrees F.

Also, grease a large rectangle dish and set aside.

In a large saucepan, add the butter, all mixed fresh herbs and garlic, cook for 6 or 7 minutes.

Add the heavy cream, the vegetables broth, salt and pepper.

Also, add the ricotta cheese and mix very well together.

Peel and slice the potatoes finely.

Place them evenly on the baking dish and pour the cream and herbs sauce on top.

Finally top it off with the grated cheese and bake in the oven for about 40 minutes or until the potatoes are soft and the cheese golden.

Recipe 16: Berries and Chocolate Cobbler

This recipe is a great dessert for the gathering of friends and family. For this recipe, I like to use caramel to enhance the sweetness of the cobbler, but in this case, chocolate is totally appropriate.

List of Ingredients:

- 2 cups fresh berries: mixed blueberries and raspberries
- 1 cup rice flour
- 1 teaspoon baking powder
- 1 teaspoon baking soda
- Pinch of salt
- ½ cup sugar
- ½ cup milk
- ¼ cup chocolate syrup or melted Nutella

Yield: 6

Cooking Time: 1 hour

AAAAAAAAAAAAAAAAAAAAAAAAAAAAAAAAAAAAAAAAAAAAAAAAAA

Instructions:

Preheat oven to 350 degrees

Grease a medium rectangle baking pan or a square one, your choice. Set aside.

In a first bowl, mix the flour, baking powder, baking soda, salt and sugar.

Add the milk and combine really well. You now have your basic batter for the cobbler.

Place all your fresh berries on the very bottom of your baking pan.

Pour the batter you prepared, on top of it.

Place in the oven and cook for about 20-25 minutes.

Remove and add the chocolate syrup or Nutella in zig zags on top of the cobbler.

Place back in the oven for another 15 minutes or so.

Serve with vanilla ice cream or whipped cream.

Recipe 17: Delicious Carrot Cupcakes

Preparing cupcakes for Easter is a wonderful idea. This dessert is my favorite and it sure will keep the children running around all day.

List of Ingredients:

- 1 cup rice flour
- 2 Tablespoons molasses
- ½ cup brown sugar
- 1 teaspoon baking powder
- 1 teaspoon baking soda
- Pinch of cinnamon
- 1 teaspoon vanilla extract
- 1 cup grated carrot
- ½ cup coconut oil (room temperature)
- 2 large eggs
- ½ cup chopped walnuts
- ½ cup applesauce

Frosting

- 1 package cream cheese (room temperature)
- 3 Tablespoons confectioner's sugar

Yield: 12

Cooking Time: 1 hour

AAAAAAAAAAAAAAAAAAAAAAAAAAAAAAAAAAAAAAAAAAAAAAAAAA

Instructions:

Preheat the oven to 350 degrees F.

Spray with non-stick oil a 12 muffins pan.

Just like most cakes, combine the dry ingredients together and the wet one separately.

Dry ingredients include: rice flour, brown sugar, baking powder, baking soda, cinnamon.

Wet ingredients include: vanilla extract, eggs, apple sauce, coconut oil, carrots.

Combine both mixtures together and add the chopped walnuts.

Pour the batter into the muffins holes and bake for 35 minutes. Meanwhile make the icing by combining the cream cheese and the confectioner's sugar.

Frost the cupcakes when they have cooled down and serve them one at a time!

Recipe 18: Fried Fish Recipe for Good Friday

If you are observing the no meat Good Friday, this fish recipe will be exactly what you need. You will be surprised by the spices I use and the wonderful taste once you pull all the ingredients together.

List of Ingredients:

- 4 grouper filets
- ½ cup quinoa flour
- 1 tablespoon cayenne pepper
- ½ teaspoons turmeric
- 1 tablespoon chili powder
- 2 eggs
- Pinch of salt
- ¼ cup. sesame oil
- ¼ cup lemon juice
- 1 tablespoon lemon zest

Yield: 4

Cooking Time: 1 hour

AAAAAAAAAAAAAAAAAAAAAAAAAAAAAAAAAAAAAAAAAAAAAAAAAAA

Instructions:

Clean each fish filet carefully and season it will salt.

In a bowl, mix the quinoa flour, turmeric, cayenne pepper and chili powder.

In a different bowl, whisk the eggs and set aside.

One filet at a time, dip it into the egg mixture and then the flour mixture to create the breading.

In a skillet, heat the sesame oil and start frying the fish filets.

It should take about 20 minutes total to cook all 4 filets, make sure your oil is really hot and that you turn the filets half way.

Serve with the lemon juice and lemon zest.

You can also use a traditional tartar sauce if you like.

Recipe 19: Bunny Eggs

These bunny eggs are cute, but also mouthwatering. You can certainly be very creative with this recipe, you can even ask the children to help out if the kitchen if they enjoy cooking. A great way to spend time with your children.

List of Ingredients:

- 12 Large Eggs
- ½ cup mayonnaise
- ¼ cup sour cream
- 1 tablespoon yellow mustard
- 1 carrot
- 1 celery stalk
- 1 green bell pepper
- Black olives
- Pinch of salt and pepper
- Smoked paprika

Yield: 24

Cooking Time: 1 hour

AAAAAAAAAAAAAAAAAAAAAAAAAAAAAAAAAAAAAAAAAAAAAAAAAA

Instructions:

The first step is of course to boil the eggs in water and salt. Once done, set them aside to let them cool down.

Cut the eggs lengthwise, and remove yolks. And place them in a separate mixing bowl.

Place the white eggs on a serving plate.

Mix the sour cream, mayonnaise, mustard and salt and pepper. Mash the egg yolks and then fill each egg white halves.

Cut the celery and green bell pepper into matchsticks.

Use them to make the bunny ears.

Cut the black olives next in small pieces and use them for the eyes.

The carrots should also be cut in matchsticks and it is to be placed as the whiskers of the bunny.

Enjoy these cute and delicious eggs!

Recipe 20: Easter Ham with An Asian Twist

It is no secret that I am a big fan of serving ham for Easter gatherings. However, over the years, I enjoyed finding new ways to prepare ham. Sure, I still enjoy serving the one with pineapple and cloves, but wait until you taste this version with an Asian twist, you will not be disappointed, I promise.

List of Ingredients:

- 5 pounds ham
- 3 Tablespoons minced fresh ginger
- 4 minced cloves garlic
- 12+ cloves
- Salt, pepper
- 1 cup vegetables broth
- 1 cup orange juice
- 1 tablespoon orange zest
- 1/3 cup honey
- ¼ cup soy sauce
- ¼ cup molasses
- 1 teaspoon cinnamon
- 1 tablespoon red pepper flakes

Yield: 6-8

Cooking Time: 2 hours

AAAAAAAAAAAAAAAAAAAAAAAAAAAAAAAAAAAAAAAAAAAAAAAAAAAA

Instructions:

Place your awesome ham in a large pot, the one that is oven safe and will allow you to add a few additional ingredients.

Preheat the oven to 400 degrees F.

In a small saucepan, mix the orange juice, vegetable broth, orange zest, soy sauce, honey and molasses. Mix and bring to a boil.

Season the ham with cinnamon, salt, pepper, ginger, garlic, red pepper flakes. Add the cloves one by one on the ham.

Finally pour the sauce you created, on top of the ham and place it in the oven.

Bake in the oven for about 2 hours. After one hour make sure you do remove the ham from the oven and pour some of the sauce back on ham to keep it moist.

If you think the ham is getting too dark, you can also cover it with foil towards the end.

Recipe 21: Small Sandwich Bites with Pickles

These yummy bites will impress even the pickiest of eaters. Be sure to choose the pickles you and your family like the best. I will mostly pick dill pickles, they are my favorite, but it is entirely up to you what kind you prefer.

List of Ingredients:

- 12 sourdough fresh slices of bread
- 6 thick smoked turkey breast
- 12 small sliced dill pickles
- ½ package roasted peppers cream cheese (also called pimento sometimes)

Yield: 24

Cooking Time: 1 hour

AAAAAAAAAAAAAAAAAAAAAAAAAAAAAAAAAAAAAAAAAAAAAAAAAAA

Instructions:

Make sure you choose very fresh and soft bread slices. You can certainly choose any type of bread you prefer for this recipe.

Cut all crusts from each bread slices. Set on a working surface.

Spread the cream cheese on all 12 slices.

Add a slice of smoked turkey on each slice followed by 2 dill pickles on 6 slices.

Cover 6 slices with turkey with the other 6 slices with only cream cheese and make the sandwiches.

Cut the sandwich into 4 and add a toothpick to each of them so the guests can grab them easily.

Recipe 22: Multicolored Macarons

My father's most favorite sweet treat were macaroons. If you would like to make them Easter appropriate, try to find some sweet candies with pastel colors to add to the recipe or use food coloring as an alternative. I prefer the candies options; since it will add some flavor and some fun to the recipe.

List of Ingredients:

- 5 cups shredded coconut
- 1 can coconut milk
- ½ cup rice flour
- 1 cup your favorite candies: chocolate chips, gummies, or even butterscotch chips if you prefer)

Yield: 36+

Cooking Time: 1 hour

AAAAAAAAAAAAAAAAAAAAAAAAAAAAAAAAAAAAAAAAAAAAAAAAAAA

Instructions:

Preheat oven to 375 degrees F.

Grease a large baking sheet and set aside.

In a bowl, mix the coconut, coconut milk, rice flour and your favorite candies.

Mix really well and form small balls, so you can drop them just as is, on the baking sheet.

Bake for about 10-12 minutes and let them cool down before tasting.

They store really well in room temperature for at least a week to 10 days.

You can also freeze them if you prefer.

Recipe 23: Scrumptious Easter Soup Idea

Do you have left over cooked ham? Then you can soon have a scrumptious warm soup to enjoy with your friends and family. Add a few veggies and your favorite broth, perhaps even split peas if you prefer.

List of Ingredients:

- 6 cups turkey broth
- 1 chopped leek
- 1 small chopped yellow onion
- 3 minced cloves garlic
- 2 cups sweet peas
- 2 Tablespoons unsalted butter
- 1 ½ cup cooked diced ham
- 2 large white potatoes
- 1 cup heavy cream
- 1 teaspoon celery salt
- Cayenne pepper
- 1 cup Gruyere cheese (shredded)

Yield: 4-5

Cooking Time: 1 hour

AAAAAAAAAAAAAAAAAAAAAAAAAAAAAAAAAAAAAAAAAAAAAAAAAAA

Instructions:

In a large pot, start by heating the butter and cooking the leek, onion and garlic for about 10 minutes.

Add the broth and the diced white potatoes. Bring to a boil and cook the potatoes until done.

Then, add the cooked diced ham, all the seasonings and sweet peas.

Continue cooking and carefully add the heavy cream.

Keep the soup simmering until almost ready to serve.

Then you can either serve the soup or add the Gruyere cheese individually on each bowl or you could decide also to place each bowl in the oven with a layer of cheese to broil.

Recipe 24: The Fun and Amazing Easter Pancakes

You must serve pancakes during the Easter break at some point right? Why not make them as fun and delicious as possible? Let's shape them like Easter eggs and the kids will gladly take a seat at the table and will possibly ask for more.

List of Ingredients:

- 2 cups all-purpose flour
- ¼ cup sugar
- 1 cup almond milk
- 1 teaspoon almond extract
- 1 teaspoon baking powder
- Unsalted butter for cooking
- 2 large eggs
- Food coloring: many colors
- Chocolate syrup
- Chocolate chips
- Whipped cream
- Sprinkles
- Confectioner's sugar

Yield: 4

Cooking Time: 40 minutes

AAAAAAAAAAAAAAAAAAAAAAAAAAAAAAAAAAAAAAAAAAAAAAAAAAAA

Instructions:

In the first bowl, mix the flour, baking powder, and sugar.

In a different bowl, combine the eggs, almond milk, and almond extract.

Then combine the dry and wet mixtures, making sure you are happy with the consistency.

Heat the butter in a small pan and start making the pancakes one at a time.

You can actually use a plastic container to design that egg shape pancakes or simply cut it into the shape you like once it's cooked.

To change things up, mix some food coloring to a few pancakes, perhaps some blue, light green or even pink.

Use the chocolate syrup, icing, and whipped cream to decorate your Easter pancakes. Having the kids help is also a great way for you to spend some more time with them.

Recipe 25: Interesting and Sweet Carrot Side Dish

Carrots are sometimes underrated. Using carrots to make a side dish is a wonderful idea because they are so nutritious and also so colorful. Don't be afraid to add some fresh herbs as toppings because they will marry beautifully with the orange color, making it look even more appetizing.

List of Ingredients:

- 3 large matchsticks carrots
- 1 chopped roughly beet
- 2 Tablespoons coconut oil
- 2 Tablespoons maple syrup
- ½ cup dry white wine
- ½ cup orange juice
- Pinch of salt and pepper
- Fresh parsley to decorate

Yield: 3-4

Cooking Time: 1 hour

AAAAAAAAAAAAAAAAAAAAAAAAAAAAAAAAAAAAAAAAAAAAAAAAAAA

Instructions:

Prepare the carrots and the beets, cutting them into matchsticks.

In a large skillet, had the coconut oil, the orange juice and wine.

Bring to a boil and add the veggies.

Cook for 15 minutes.

Then, add the maple syrup, salt and pepper and combine well.

Serve when you are satisfied with how crunchy or soft the veggies are. Garnish with fresh parsley.

About the Author

Molly Mills always knew she wanted to feed people delicious food for a living. Being the oldest child with three younger brothers, Molly learned to prepare meals at an early age to help out her busy parents. She just seemed to know what spice went with which meat and how to make sauces that would dress up the blandest of pastas. Her creativity in the kitchen was a blessing to a family where money was tight and making new meals every day was a challenge.

Molly was also a gifted athlete as well as chef and secured a Lacrosse scholarship to Syracuse University. This was a blessing to her family as she was the first to go to college and at little cost to her parents. She took full advantage of her college education and earned a business degree. When she graduated, she joined her culinary skills and business acumen into a successful catering business. She wrote her first e-book after a customer asked if she could pay for several of her recipes. This sparked the entrepreneurial spirit in Mills and she thought if one person wanted them, then why not share the recipes with the world!

Molly lives near her family's home with her husband and three children and still cooks for her family every chance she gets. She plays Lacrosse with a local team made up of her old teammates from college and there are always some tasty nibbles on the ready after each game.

Don't Miss Out!

Scan the QR-Code below and you can sign up to receive emails whenever Molly Mills publishes a new book. There's no charge and no obligation.

Sign Me Up

https://molly.gr8.com

Made in the USA
Middletown, DE
09 April 2020